CW00819616

SELECTED POEMS

Also by Mimi Khalvati

Persian Miniatures
In White Ink
Mirrorwork
Entries on Light

Tying the Song
(co-edited with Pascale Petit)

MIMI KHALVATI

SELECTED POEMS

CARCANET

First published in 2000 by
Carcanet Press Limited
4th Floor, Conavon Court
12-16 Blackfriars Street
Manchester M3 5BQ

Copyright © Mimi Khalvati 1991, 1995, 1997, 2000

The right of Mimi Khalvati to be identified
as the author of this work has been asserted
by her in accordance with the Copyright,
Designs and Patents Act of 1988
All rights reserved

A CIP catalogue record for this book
is available from the British Library
ISBN 1 85754 472 2

The publisher acknowledges financial assistance
from the Arts Council of England

Set in 10pt Garamond Simoncini by Bryan Williamson, Frome
Printed and bound in England by SRP Ltd, Exeter

Contents

6

from In White Ink

In women's speech, as in their writing, that element which never stops resonating . . . is the song: first music from the first voice of love which is alive in every woman . . . A woman is never far from 'mother' . . . There is always within her at least a little of that good mother's milk. She writes in white ink.

Hélène Cixous, The Laugh of the Medusa

The Woman in the Wall

Why they walled her up seems academic.
They have their reasons. She was a woman
with a nursing child. Walled she was
and dying. But even when they surmised

there was nothing of her left but dust and ghost
at dawn, at dusk, at intervals
the breast recalled, wilful as the awe
that would govern village lives, her milk flowed.

And her child suckled at the wall, drew
the sweetness from the stone and grew
till the cracks knew only wind and weeds
and she was weaned. Centuries ago.

Stone of Patience

'In the old days,' she explained to a grandchild
bred in England, 'in the old days in Persia
it was the custom to have a stone, a special stone
you would keep to talk to, tell your troubles to,
a stone we called, as they now call me, a stone of patience.'

No therapists then to field a question with another
but stones from dust where ladies' fingers, cucumbers
curled in sun. Were the ones they used for gherkins
babies that would have grown, like piano tunes had we known
the bass beyond the first few bars? Or miniatures?

Some things I'm content to guess – colour in a crocus-tip,
is it gold or mauve? A girl or a boy . . . Patience
was so simple then, waiting for the clematis to open,
to purple on a wall, the bud to shoot out stamens,
the jet of milk to leave its rim like honey on the bee's fur.

But patience when the cave is sealed, a boulder
at the door, is riled by the scent of hyacinth
in the blue behind the stone: a willow by the pool
where once she sat to trim a beard with kitchen scissors,
to tilt her hat at smiles, sleep, congratulations.

And a woman faced with a lover grabbing for his shoes
when women friends would have put themselves in hers
no longer knows what's virtuous. Will anger
shift the boulder, buy her freedom and the earth's?
Or patience like the earth's be abused? Even nonchalance

can lead to courage, conception: a voice that says
oh come on darling, it'll be alright, oh do let's.
How many children were born from words such as these?
I know my own were, now learning to repeat them,
to outgrow a mother's awe of consequence her body bears.

So now that midsummer, changing shape, has brought in
another season, the grape becoming raisin, hinting
in a nip at the sweetness of a clutch, one fast upon another;
now that the breeze is raising sighs from sheets
as she tries to learn again, this time for herself,

to fling caution to the winds or to borrow patience
from the stones in her own backyard where fruit
still hangs on someone else's branch, don't ask her
whose? as if it mattered. Say *they won't mind*
as you reach for a leaf, for the branch, and pull it down.

Family Footnotes

My arms in the sink, I half-listen
as someone keeps me company.
She's such a sweetiepie, isn't she?
I pause and to my own surprise

realise, seeing her suddenly through the eyes
of guests, how small she seems;
like a robin redbreast perched with other
mothers I thank god aren't mine.

My father cracks a joke on the transatlantic
line, misreading my alliances;
decades of regret still failing
to make her an easy butt.

But his laugh is warm bubble, a devil
to slip into, like the fold of his cheek
and the grey ring round his eye
my own before long will look through.

My children are with me as always, my son
even now sleeping under covers
I have no more to do with. He is always
loving. To say this, think this

seems suspect in a world such as ours.
How have we escaped it?
My daughter is about to bumble in the door,
late as usual, and be sweet to me,

nattering on as I clatter in the kitchen,
her breasts within an inch of my arm.
Nothing seems to rattle her – embarrassments
that floor me, still, at my age.

She is chock-a-block with courage;
fresh air on her cheeks like warpaint.
Pooled in this – this love – and this and this –
what has riddled me to long for more?

Shanklin Chine

It surfaces at moments, unlooked-for,
when the little crooked child appears
to bar your way: demanding no crooked
sixpence as she stands behind the stile
in her little gingham frock and the blood
she has in mind drawn behind her gaze.

Are you the guardian of the Chine?
(Perhaps she needs some recognition.)
Of course she never talks.
She only has the one face – dark and solemn,
the one stance – blackboard-set
and a wit as nimble as the Chine

stopping short at forgiveness
that could only come with time or power
or a body large enough to fit her brain.
Is there something I could give her?
Some blow to crack her ice,
human warmth to make her feel the same?

Genie of the Chine, she reappears at moments
when I am closest to waterways, underworlds,
little crooked streams through hemlock
and dandelion that end so prematurely –
though *she* is there, like Peter Pan,
or the barbed-wire children who bang tin cans

or the child you would have loved
like any mother, any father, had you been
an adult, not the child with no demands
for sixpences in puddings, pumpkins
on the table or any pumpkin pies gracing
homes that had you standing at their gates.

Genie of the Chine, she reappears
from time to time, when I am closest to myself.

Sick Boy

In the shallow, like a dog, between the sideboard
and the sound of breaking water,
his fear curls.

From the high road by the stove
whose smoke is scenting speed
outside his travel –

Swish! a figure stooping
in the corner rinses fruit
beyond the peel,

places three magic colours,
dots, a water-wand to name them
by a bowl of tangerines.

Under the covers it locks him in:
the rod, the rail, the storm.
Oh Mum. The sea.

Sand trails off the shells,
feet going down, the brambles'
pale green store.

Blue Moon

Sitting on a windowsill, swinging
her heels against the wall as the gymslips
circled round and Elvis sang *Blue Moon,*

she never thought one day to see her daughter,
barelegged, sitting crosslegged on saddlebags
that served as sofas, pulling on an ankle

as she nodded sagely, smiling, not denying –
you'll never catch me dancing to the same old tunes;
while her brother, strewed along a futon,

grappled with his Sinclair, setting up
a programme we'd asked him to. Tomorrow
he would teach us how to use it but for now

he lay intent, pale, withdrawn, peripheral
in its cold white glare as we went up to our rooms:
rooms we once exchanged, like trust, or guilt,

each knowing hers would serve the other better
while the other's, at least for now, would do.
The house is going on the market soon.

My son needs higher ceilings; and my daughter
sky for her own blue moon. You can't blame her.
No woman wants to dance in her Mum's old room.

The Bowl

The path begins to climb the hills that confine the lake-basin. The ascent is steep and
joyless; but it is as nothing compared with the descent on the other side, which is long,
precipitous, and inconceivably nasty. This is the famous Kotal-i-Pir-i-Zan, or Pass of the
Old Woman.
    Some writers have wondered at the origin of the name. I feel no such surprise . . .
For, in Persia, if one aspired, by the aid of a local metaphor, to express anything that
was peculiarly uninviting, timeworn, and repulsive, a Persian old woman would be the
first and most forcible simile to suggest itself. I saw many hundreds of old women . . . in
that country . . . and I crossed the Kotal-i-Pir-i-Zan, and I can honestly say that whatever
derogatory or insulting remarks the most copious of vocabularies might be capable of
expending upon the one, could be transferred, with equal justice, to the other.
    . . . At the end of the valley the track . . . discloses a steep and hideous descent,
known to fame, or infamy, as the Kotal-i-Dokhter, or Pass of the Maiden.
    . . . As I descended the Daughter, and alternately compared and contrasted her
features with those of the Old Woman, I fear that I irreverently paraphrased a well-
known line,
O matre laeda filia laedior!
                    George Nathaniel Curzon, *Persia and the Persian Question* (1892)

i

The bowl is big and blue. A flash of leaf
along its rim is green, spring-green, lime
and herringbone. Across the glaze where fish swim,
over the loose-knit waves in hopscotch-black,

16

borders of fish-eye and cross-stitch, chestnut trees
throw shadows: candles, catafalques and barques
and lord knows what, what ghost of ancient seacraft,
what river-going name we give to shadows.

Inside the bowl where clay has long since crusted,
under the dust and loam, leaf forms lie
fossilized. They have come from mountain passes,
orchards where no water runs, stony tracks
with only threadbare shade for mares and mule foals.
They are named: cuneiform and ensiform,
spathulate and sagittate and their margins
are serrated, lapidary, lobed.

My book of botany is green: the gloss
of coachpaint, carriages, Babushka dolls,
the clouded genie jars of long ago.
Inside my bowl a womb of air revolves.
What tadpole of the margins, holly-spine
of seahorse could be nosing at its shallows,
what honeycomb of sunlight, marbled green
of malachite be cobbled in its hoop?

I squat, I stoop. My knees are either side
of bowl. My hands are eyes around its crescent.
The surface of its story feathers me,
my ears are wrung with rumour. On a skyline
I cannot see a silhouette carves vase-shapes
into sky: baby, belly, breast, thigh;
an aeroplane I cannot hear has shark fins
and three black camels sleep in a blue, blue desert.

ii

My bowl has cauled my memories. My bowl
has buried me. Hoofprints where Ali's horse
baulked at the glint of cutlasses have thrummed
against my eyelids. Caves where tribal women
stooped to place tin sconces, their tapers lit,
have scaffolded my skin. Limpet-pools
have scooped my gums, raising weals and the blue
of morning-glory furled around my limbs.

17

My bowl has smashed my boundaries: harebell
and hawthorn mingling in my thickened waist
of jasmine; catkin and *chenar*,* dwarf-oak
and hazel hanging over torrents, deltas,
my seasons' arteries . . . *Lahaf-Doozee!* . . .
My retina is scarred with shadow-dances
and echoes run like hessian blinds across
my sleep; my ears are niches, prayer-rug arches.

Lahaf-Doozee! My backbone is an alley,
a one-way runnelled alley, cobblestoned
with hawkers' cries, a saddlebag of ribs.
The Quilt Man comes. He squats, stoops, tears strips
of flattened down, unslings his pole of heartwood
and plucks the string: *dang dang tok tok* and cotton
jumping, jumping, leaps to the twang of thread,
leaping, flares in a cloudy hill of fleece.

My ancestors have plumped their quilts with homespun,
in running-stitch have handed down their stories:
an infant in its hammock, safe in cloud,
who swung between two walls an earthquake spared,
hung swaying to and fro, small and holy.
Lizards have kept their watch on lamplight, citrus-
peel in my mother's hand becoming baskets.
My bowl beneath the tap is scoured with leaves.

iii

The white rooms of the house we glimpsed through pine,
quince and pomegranate are derelict.
Calendars of saint-days still cling to plaster,
drawing-pinned. Velvet-weavers, hammam-keepers
have rolled their weekdays in the rags, the closing
craft-bag of centuries. And worker bees
on hillsides, hiding in ceramic jars,
no longer yield the gold of robbers' honey.

---

* *Chenar*: plane-tree

High on a ledge, a white angora goat bleats . . .
I too will take my bowl and leave these wheatfields
speckled with hollyhocks, campanulas,
the threshing-floors on roofs of sundried clay.
Over twigbridge, past camel-thorn and thistle
bristling with snake, through rock rib and ravine
I will lead my mule to the high ground, kneel
above the eyrie, spread my rug in shade.

Below me, as the sun goes down, marsh pools
will glimmer red. *Sineh Sefid** will be gashed
with gold, will change from rose to blue, from blue
to grey. My bowl will hold the bowl of sky
and as twilight falls I will stand and fling
its spool and watch it land as lake: a ring
where *rood* and *river* meet in peacock-blue
and peacock-green and a hundred rills cascade.

And evening's narrow pass will bring me down
to bowl, to sit at lakeside's old reflections:
those granite spurs no longer hard and cold
but furred in the slipstream of a lone oarsman.
And from its lap a scent will rise like Mer†
from mother-love and waters; scent whose name
I owe to *Talat, gold* for grandmother:
Maryam, tuberose, for bowl, for daughter.

---

* *Sineh Sefid*: Mt. White Breast
† *Mer*: Egyptian goddess of mother-love and waters

Rubaiyat
for Telajune

Beyond the view of crossroads ringed with breath
her bed appears, the old-rose covers death
has smoothed and stilled; her fingers lie inert,
her nail-file lies beside her in its sheath.

The morning's work over, her final chore
was 'breaking up the sugar' just before
siesta, sitting crosslegged on the carpet,
her slippers lying neatly by the door.

The image of her room behind the pane,
though lost as the winding road shifts its plane,
returns on every straight, like signatures
we trace on glass, forget and find again.

I have inherited her tools: her anvil,
her axe, her old scrolled mat, but not her skill;
and who would choose to chip at sugar-blocks
when sugar-cubes are boxed beside the till?

The scent of lilacs from the road reminds me
of my own garden: a neighbouring tree
grows near the fence. At night its clusters loom
like lantern-moons, pearly-white, unearthly.

I don't mind that the lilac's roots aren't mine.
Its boughs are, and its blooms. It curves its spine
towards my soil and litters it with dying
stars: deadheads I gather up like jasmine.

My grandmother would rise and take my arm,
then sifting through the petals in her palm
would place in mine the whitest of them all:
'Salaam, dokhtaré-mahé-man, salaam!'

'Salaam, my daughter-lovely-as-the-moon!'
Would that the world could see me, Telajune,
through your eyes! Or that I could see a world
that takes such care to tend what fades so soon.

20

Earls Court

I brush my teeth harder when the gum bleeds.
Arrive alone at parties, leaving early.

The tide comes in, dragging my stare
from pastures I could call my own.

Through the scratches on the record – *Ah! Vieni, vieni!** –
I concentrate on loving.

I use my key. No duplicate of this.
Arrive alone at parties, leaving early.

I brush my teeth harder when the gum bleeds.
Sing to the fern in the steam. Not even looking –

commuters buying oranges, Italian vegetables,
bucket flowers from shores I might have danced in, briefly.

I use my key – a lost belonging on the stair.
Sing to the fern in the steam. I wash my hair.

The tide goes out, goes out. The body's wear and tear.
Commuters' faces turn towards me: bucket flowers.

A man sits eyeing destinations on the train.
He wears Islamic stubble, expensive clothes, two rings.

He talks to himself in Farsi, loudly like a drunk.
Laughs aloud to think where life has brought him.

Eyeing destinations on the train – a lost belonging –
talks to himself with a laugh I could call my own.

Like a drunk I want to neighbour him, sit beside
his stubble's scratch, turn his talking into chatting.

I want to tell him I have a ring like his,
only smaller. I want to see him use his key.

---

* From Puccini's *Madama Butterfly*

21

I want to hear the child who runs to him call
Baba! I want to hear him answer, turning

from his hanging coat: *Beeya, Babajune, beeya!*
Ah! Vieni, vieni! . . .

In Lieu of a Postcard

What is it that your absences have nursed
in me? What 'quiet grove'? What 'dreamy view'?
No odyssey perfects those scenes of you
I ramble in, rehearsed and re-rehearsed.
No information bureau better-versed
in catalogue, no lace whose cutwork grew
in shocks of spider-margarita dew*
can map my moods' terrain, its pocks of thirst.
And only habit, yours. I wonder if,
late at night, the cricket over, a criss-
cross rain outside is drumming while you snooze;
and wake to closing scores to find its riff
reminds you, not of deadlines you may miss,
but songlines more insistent than the blues'.

Jasmine

If you find
the end of the root
in the scent of jasmine
and bind it through

till your sight
is amnesia
and your breath
love's wound,

---

* Spider-margarita: a traditional pattern in Cypriot lace

you will wake with blossoms
starring your hair,
the will
to live more sweetly

girdling you
in ebbing rings
like Titania
smiling at an ass.

Rice

i

Ten years later, I recognise his profile in a Tehran cab.
You see these teeth, he says, leaning across the passengers,
what became of me? . . . I see him silhouetted in dazzle
as the tunnel ends on the last lap to Frankfurt, his hand
on the window's metal lip, his cap in the other circling
like a bird then, loosed on the wind, beating a tattoo

against the wires as I watch him reach to the rack for his case,
send that, too, struggling through the window, socks and all.
I have come, he declared, *to start at the start!* Now, a decade
later, he asks: *You see these teeth?* He bares them in the light
to show how short, how straight they are. *What became of me:
you wonder why?* His fist emerges from his pocket, clenched.

*I eat it all the time. My hand is never still, like a swallow
at its nest, going in, going out. Not a grain escapes.*
He fingers his moustache. *I even check in wing-mirrors.
See how it's worn my teeth right down?* His hand unfurls,
dabs at the row of laps between us. *Please, have some.*
What, raw? I ask. *It's rice,* he urges. *Rice.*

ii

I have fled on mules, the star of Turkey in my sky, to start
at the start. I have come like sleet with Mary in the dark, swum
into hedgerows by the line. Gifts of weave and leather tucked
in polythene for friends, already fled or free, are dry.
Will they harbour us, we wonder, ten years, a revolution later,
towel us from swollen rivers chanting MARG BAR EMRIKA*?

iii

The cabs still carry passengers: my mother in her black chador,
my sisters among soldiers, now and then a face
pulped like a cake. They have granted me asylum. I write plays.
A friend I love in London has hung the Kurdish mules I brought her
on the same hook as an old sitar she never plays.
When she dusts them she thinks of me, and of rivers.

I told her of the man I met twice: once in a train,
once again in Tehran in those early days . . . what days they were!
Ah well. Her sister lives near Washington where the husband
works for the Department of Defence, and in real estate; comes home
to scan *The Post*, its leaders on Japan: po-faced as she snatches
victory from jaws set ever closer as they wing towards Potomac.

Baba Mostafa

He circles slowly and the walls of the room,
this Maryland cocoon, swirl as though the years
were not years but faces and he, at eighty,
in his warm woolly robe, were the last slow waltz.

'Children,' he would say, '*truly* love me!
And I have always, always loved children.'
'It's true,' she'd say, coming through the arch.
'Sarajune, you love Baba Mostafa, don't you?

---

* Death to America

24

D'you love Baba Mostafa or Maman Gitty, hah?
Here, eat this.' 'For God's sake, woman,
do you want her to choke! Come, Sarajune, dance . . .
da-dum, da-dum, da-dum, da-da . . .'

He circles slowly, the child on his shoulder
nestled like a violin and the ruches of a smile
on the corners of his lips as though the babygro'
beneath his hand were glissades of satin.

'Wunderschön! Das ist wunderschön!' He lingers
on the umlaut he learned as a student on a scholarship
from Reza Shah and on the lips of a Fräulein
whose embouchure lives on in him, takes him back
through all those years, through marriages, children,
reversals of fortune, remembering how in wartime
foodstuffs left his home for hers – manna from Isfahan,
sweetmeats from Yazd, dried fruit from Azarbaijan.

He circles slowly, on paisley whorls
that once were cypress-trees bowing to the wind,
as though these 'perfect moslems' were reflections
of his coat-tails lifting on a breeze from the floor.

'I swear to God,' he blubbered, only days before
his laryngotomy, 'I was a good man. I never stole.
And if – and who can say? – you never had the father
my other children had, God knows it wasn't in my hands.'
'How is he?' they whispered in doorways as I buried
my butt-ends in beds of azaleas. Months later,
he writes: 'I can't eat *gut* and sleep *gut*.' He never could:
holding up *Der Spiegel*, in the small hours, to the lamp.

And now he circles, from room to room,
with a grandchild for company who step by step
outstrips him as he learns – re-learns – to talk . . .
da-dum, da-dum, da-dum, da-da . . .

Haiku

On the verandah
the wet-nurse thinks of her own
pomegranate tree.

from Mirrorwork

From *Mirrorwork*
for Archie

Of course the serendipity of it moved me:
    a mirror-tree as metaphor become a
    mirror-tree as mural; a cherry outside
    my window become a willow in a tableau.
    The real become imaginal and vice versa.

Fooled me into forgetting, as I stopped just
    past the newsagent's on sunny days to
    see it glitter, how excitement tempered
    by dismay had first become, like the tree,
    asymmetrical.

Dismayed not so much that the willow-tree of
    England should deck itself in mirrorwork
    but that mirrorwork should lend itself to
    partwork, the inextricability of light
    and shade compromised by paint, ceramic,
    broken tile, glass used as decoration.

It marks the Silver Jubilee 1977. Below
    the roofline is captioned: THE ISLAND.
    I know nothing more about it. The area
    is still new to me but, as the mirror-
    tree seemed to suggest, somewhere to
    come home to on my own terms.

You know all this, or some of it. Who
    never asked of me a poem but a dedication.

*

You know half the story: the mirror side
    that glitters. But the cherry-tree
    in Highgate fed through all those years
    with blank looks behind glass, my smoke,
    your smokescreens, silences disclaiming
    even argument – you never knew how I
    gendered her, mirrored her.

She hangs my bedroom lights like globes
    against her throat, recycles snow as
    blossom when I am retrograde with
    childhood, still wearing winter clothes

and like a jaded lover levelling eyes across
    a road, cares little how I summer, what
    ornamental fruit I find to match her own.

I saw in her indifference yours. In her
    blossoms my bitterness at England. I
    never saw the cherry-tree. I'm not
    interested in trees. But in matching
    your indifference.

I refuse the natural detail to tell you how
    things look, how sky would look without a
    tree to blot my view of an avenue through
    cloudbanks like the genie from the bonfire
    growing longer, quieter, skyward.

                        *

Standing in its plot, its absence of a
    paving stone, my cherry-tree dissembles
    intimacy in echoes, seasons I think
    mirror me like the bric-à-brac of homes
    that took me in but were not mine

though I knew as well as they where biscuits,
    string or dog-lead lived and could be
    seen by strangers walking past at a
    dresser, drawer, brutally at home in
    the world as any back view in a window

or frontal view of cherry, dogged as a
    greeting card with yet another Eden,
    yet another plot of fruit, cat, bird.

You chose red for the bedroom carpet.
  How were you to know how much there
  was already in duvet, pillow, curtain,
  kimono? How was I to know, agreeing,
  the fights ahead?

                              *

I've curtained off the tree today,
  pretending that her half of sky is
  greyer, wetter, more opaque. The
  half I see through, where no tree is,
  is lighter, actual.

My mother has gone on a coach trip with
  the Royal Academy and of course it's
  pouring down with rain. Her glasses,
  some days dark and some days clear,
  are pressed against a dream of heat
  behind the pane.

Beyond this cul-de-sac is a no man's land
  where a clutch of trees in shade, water
  in a bucket still rocking from the rhythm
  of a back that halts to stretch, droplets
  on a forearm shimmering with pinpoint suns
  reclaim

energies of land, water, sun from scrutiny,
  assert their own economy, impervious as
  nature is to human dialogue and pain.

My tree is nothing but the thought of something
  not itself: a bare land that throws its
  own desire for shadow, orchard, rain.

                              *

I used to look for you in books, divine you
in Susan Griffin's WOMAN AND NATURE, *find*
you in MATTER, SEPARATION (Where He Begins).

I'd close my eyes, place thumbs against the
first half (where I knew you were), will you
out of the margins of this strange I Ching.

Mathematician, archaeologist, astronomer,
something to do with husbandry, marquetry,
dressage, optics, you were all these things.
You spoke in number, weight, measure, myth,
from chambers, mooncraters, 'time itself,
gathering speed'. Your tools were bronze,
their points fine as pins.

Once in a blue moon you were soft and vul-
nerable, 'one hand awake even in sleep'.

*

When sun promises a patch of sky bluer
   than the rest, I remember as a child
   looking up at sky, never seeing the
   legs around me, things tied to earth,

faces of carol singers, chapel readers
   oblivious to the company of angels.

Always above, beyond, were pathways of
   desire rising like lost balloons ever
   higher, higher. On an ottoman of cloud
   were no Gods, Kings, Olympians, but
   old men none the less, in cloth of gold
   with fruit and feast ranged in a
   long, light wait.

Walking back from playing-fields with vows
   held like bonfire heat warm inside my
   blazer, I would then see, as if for
   the first time, figures round me,

alpines, flaking bark and place myself,
   precise as any living thing, among them.

*

Where has it gone, the eye to eye, flank
   to flank, the same word of the same
   sentence said together, stopped together,
   unseeingness of arms around, eyes behind
   each other's backs?

A boy from Basra, numbed and in a cell
   too dark to see, imagining that he'd lost
   his arms, kept asking where they had
   taken them, kept asking where we keep them.

Where, in a world we take apart, a world
   we cannot share, imagining we might see
   ourselves in him and him in us, might
   use our arms to hold him, touch his own
   and tell him . . .

But it's we who are in the dark. We
   are the thought of something not itself.
   Each fragment whole, each unit split, but
   dovetailed, one wall, one dome in whose
   muddied lakes of colour swim the blues
   of a bag, green rings of a skirt.

We are the hall of mirrors, fine mosaic,
   the mirrorwork in which not even Kings
   can see themselves.

*

Yards from the mural, through the trees:
glimmerings of silver, glints you might
mistake for sunlight on a frontispiece,
optical illusions.

Disclosed, willow branches bifurcate into
angels' wings, epaulettes amassing,
dripping silver.

Look up close: back into its splintered
eyes! Retinas of leaf look back at you
in unison. Living green in painted,
living eyes in eye-slits. Voices
thrown, disowned. Ventriloquism.

Tree in glass recoils from you, leans to
orbit, stars. Shine without reflection.

A celebration. Faded to a fresco by
breakage, refuse, accident. Pick one
mosaic: crock from Turkey, blue on white,
shop-surround in Ankara, Stoke Newington.

Hair of waterfall on brick, leaf-flèche, braid.
There's no escaping silver. Mercury's
plunge downwards. Running crests that
leap: *The Great Wave off Kanazawa*.

A sea so bright with moonshine that it blinds
its own horizon. Awed at the power of
motion. The power of awe to still an ocean.

*

Under the green canopy are painted locals,
mostly children, festive at a table.
In geometrics – jellies, cakes, the usual
bright concoctions. A photographer,
black-suited, unnaturally large, with his
right arm raised. Two boys with a spade.

CLEARING THE RUBBISH NOV 78, lettered on
 a wheelbarrow, stirs a memory of people
 who, catalogue to hand, armed with captions,
 dates, visit galleries and gardens asking
 factual questions, filling in the context.
 The English are good at this. Iranians
 hopeless.

Coming upon mirrorwork in Hackney, my father,
 for example, might shake his head (denoting
 in Iran admiration), note differences between
 theirs and ours – mirrorsmiths, community –
 and feel, without expressing it, a severance,
 a loss of context.

Around the corner from behind his shop-window,
 the dry-cleaner waves to someone passing.
 No one looks at the mirror-tree. It has
 grown on them, from birth for some, drained
 its dazzle into eyes grown tired of dazzle.

I glance as I pass. Not with indifference
 but an incipient sense of the customary.
 Seeing things as they are. You, me.
 Accommodating difference. On its own terms.

Vine-Leaves

Even the vine-leaves shot with sun
have shadow leaves
pressed close on them.

Even the vine is hanging
ones that seem like twos:
a top leaf
on a shadow leaf, its corner slipped,
like invoices in duplicate.

If I stood to look from the other side
with the light behind me,
would I still not see
how the top leaf shot with sun
might be the one that fails to fit
its duplicate

instead of
– standing where I do – seeing
how it is the shadow leaf that fails to fit
and failing

makes the one leaf seem like two
and being two, more beautiful?

What Seemed so Quiet

when I listen hard
is bird to bird, wheel on rain,
what you say, I say.

How tall the pines are!
Heads thinned as though to hear what
heaven says through wind.

The harder grey falls
the brighter grows the dream of
light, and wind (like rain

that is only heard
as it meets our world on water,
stone or pane), wind

itself a silent
thing you think would drown you out
well might, but also

carries you the more
to blow through open windows
like my own, in Highgate.

The North-Facing Garden
for Jill

I have never seen her in the garden.
Never heard her gardening. Only heard her
talk of moonlight walks, perhaps tonight
if the clouds clear.

I have heard no one in the garden.
Heard nothing but the waterfall, fountain,
the pitter-patter in steamrise, after rainfall,
that dribbles off at seven.

Yet someone must have gardened it. Hours
every day for years. The evidence is there –
barrow, cuttings, a ladder in the wood – someone
who did it all before we came.

Like the Indians before Columbus.
Like nature before woman stepped,
hair dripping like a seal, with her infant
out of water.

Or the invisible footmen of our childhoods,
shadow hands that served us, we
who were Beauty at the table of the Beast
we also were.

Here, shadows are where colour grows
though only rose, all shades of rose
from the palest of anemone to the reds of dogwood,
wedlock – the rose itself.

The garden facing North takes its colour
not from sun but from her face: deepening
in the evenings, stove-flushed, lamplit, waking
to a bedroom facing West –

Why I'm no good in the mornings, she says.
Behind the eyes, smile, dip and rise of features
that apologise for the poverty of words,
stones speak, spirits prove

and with time on her hands, she makes Eden hers:
re-entering through a backdoor stone-propped open,
unseen behind an arch, hovering like a shade
of our former selves.

Writing in the Sun

is a kind of blindness:
blinded by the sun
and blinded in the shade

in a vague abstractedness to leaf
– like a library of words
heard dimly or forgotten –

writing in the sun
is what would make

re-entering a room
as cool, hushed
as walking into sleep

if sleep were
a marble void
on the threshold of cathedrals.

For a moment it seemed easier
to walk towards the park
purposeless

than to take my life in hand,
become, if only for an instant,
someone writing in the sun

when one instance of imagining
walking into people's prayers
might be answered
with another and another.

Prayer

has nothing of the grandeur
or the violence of crowds
but circles stockinged
in its own quiet sphere

like lamplight sealing off gloom
by its cone against the dark,
an interval when weightless

the body loses cut and thrust,
rises like a plume of smoke
to add its grievances to air's.

Prayer
is like watering the plants,
popping out to get the paper,
a trundling, pottering,

an audience for dust
that settles even as the duster's hand
moves across the grain.

Prayer can interrupt itself – fling
instructions over a shoulder, offer
delicacies on a shelf;

resume itself, its murmuring
like berries, herbs
left drying in the sun

as moving out of earshot
you find your own momentum,
your freedom not to pray.

Prayer is not a scourge.
Thought the head bows, back stoops,
it's a lifting, a soft and drifting
spiral like the echoes of a string plucked,

a sky to feel alone in,
how small one is, how packed
the earth with people,

how far the neighbour's radio
– as brow meets stone – recedes
and amber beads count amber suns
that are still to rise, still to set.

Prayer is a time of day
that on a winding stair
greets itself.

Needlework

Inside the lamplight's circle,
in the embroidery hoop the flowers,
my name within my lifetime
handed on to no one dies with me.

My knots are neat.
My cottage gardens will be stretched
with the ones my daughters stitch.
My youngest keeps me company.

On an upper landing where my work
is hung, in another century,
some strange and foreign woman
may try to picture me

and fail. Or is it that I fail
to picture her? I cannot think
what she would want with me.
With hollyhocks and bonnets.

From *Interiors*
after Edouard Vuillard

Edouard Vuillard (1868-1940) lived with his mother until her death when he was 50. Mme. Vuillard was a seamstress and her workroom, like his studio, was part of the home. 'The home and the studio were one, and the honour of the home and the honour of the studio the same honour. What resulted? Everything was a rhythm, a rite and a ceremony from the moment of rising. Everything was a sacred event . . .'

(Charles Péguy, l'Argent)

THE PARLOUR

Between cup and lip,
needle and cloth,
the closing of a cupboard door
and reassertion of a room,

in those pauses when the head lifts
and time stands still

what gesture slips its epoch
to evoke another continent?
What household conjures household

in the homogeneity of furniture,
rituals that find their choirs
in morning light, evening lamps,
cloths and clothes and screens?

This woman sewing,
man reading at his desk,
in raising eyes towards the wall
do they lose themselves in foliage,

sense themselves receding
to become presences on gravel paths
and in becoming incorporeal
free to be transposed?

Do they see themselves and not themselves
– have any sense how manifold
might be their incarnations –
in the needlepoint of walls and skies
so distant from their own?

For this profile hazed
against shutterfold and sky
has as many claimants
as there are flowers on the wall,
in a vase, on a dress, in the air

and everywhere, like leaves,
recognitions drop their calling-cards
on a mood, a table set for supper,

disperse themselves as freely
as the mille-fleurs from a palette,

settle unobtrusively
as her to her sewing, him to his book,
lowering eyes from vistas
that have brought them to themselves.

THE WORKROOM

It was in the whirring of a treadle,
biting of a thread,
resumption of the treadle

while eyes were closed
and shadows of the scissors
like the noon sun through its zenith
were passing overhead

that allegiances were fed their rhythms,
loyalties first given shape.

With a lever sprung, a length released,
launched in its wake on a sea of stuffs,
flecks of wool, waves of walnut grain,

given food and drink, we gave
the thanks we never knew in time
we would strive to give, to keep alive
in words, in songs, in paint.

It was in these gestures, the day's devotions,
with a pockmarked thumb, pinheads
jammed in a mouth that held them safe,
that an inheritance was slowly stitched,

a paradigm to give body to
like a second life to curtains,
lining to a dress. And now
when prayers we never knew were prayers

in the guise of silver bobbins,
machines we never mastered,
are once again at work
in the hands of daughters making light

of the partnering, unpartnering of threads;
when voices caught then thought lost
in transit while ours in vows
were still keeping faith

return in transpositions
in a dream like a revelation,
familial as they were in life
to orchestrate our states of grace,

how can we not fail them?
What sacraments can we find but these
poor leavings of a memory
of a home, a time, a place?

STUDIES FOR THE WORKROOM

With an arm along a table,
a head against an arm
and the sensation of an eye

from the highest corner of the room
that looks down, sees only

our right side laid
in folds of light
while shadows on its underside
pulsate against an ear

how childhood in its timelessness
like a fishspine between sun and moon

in this laying out of halves,
this pool of concentricity,
luxuriates!

*

While journeys made
are left hanging in their harbours,
hanging in farewells,

journeys daydreams sail on
surprise themselves with atolls:
an atoll in an Indian ocean

where birds that have lost their power of flight
because they have no enemies

make scissor-runs across sand and tide –
poignant, being flightless,
more poignant, being safe.

*

Through banging in the kitchen,
cousins' voices drifting
out of space, through liquid

slugging into jugs
and the smell of olive oil
– tomato pips like frogspawn
pooled on small glass plates –

comes the punctuation of a reverie,
a summons arcing over chairs.

A disc of air, bright or warm
to walk towards

forms when they call one's name.

*

But where, among figures stooping, stretching
in tigerstripes and polka-dots,
women flattened into vase-shapes,
waisted into drapes,

women always floor-length
whose elbows might be objects,
objects hair,

where is the figure centre-stage,
actor with his laughlines,
critic with his tabby cat,

the great divide
from which all distances, certainties
irradiate?

Here are two heads at an angle,
one woman cutting cloth
and both heads at an angle that suggests

an intimacy, rapport,
a solicitude

but may only be the one
from which
they see straight.

*

Drops of sweat fall on lawn, go grey
and white again under the iron's nose
as steam clears.

It clears on fields
sewn one to another,
braided with a hedge.

On the far side of the hedge
is nothing:
no life except one's own,
the sky's, trees', clouds',

nothing where ought to be
the promise that was given
when one thought of looking there.

Tacking in an armhole
flashes semaphore and sunray.

*

Out in the park it's lighter
than it was, lighter than expected
as though the afternoon
had reversed itself.

But here indoors, we're solid
as clocktime, any segment of a day,
any going in and out of rooms
that hold each other's voices
on the measures of a thread.

Over doorsills, tiles,
from the intensity of borders
to the middle ground and back again,
taking carpets at their own speed,
we move along their pathways;

ducking under tape measures,
even out of earshot, not alone.
And tonight, in our room,
when voices silent in the thick of walls
talk among themselves we will feel,

lodged long before we enter,
like a bass note to the streetlight,
a memory forgotten that will not go away,

the ceiling of a presence,
a company, a solitude,

like hearing in the dark
intermittent rain.

*

Once the wheel is turned,
articulations of the lever
folded under cover for the night

and the need for counting stops
as blankets open up their triangles,
tartan rugs their squares,

those whose closing eyes rely
on an eye that keeps its vigil
empowered in the dark to see
brighter in their stead, know,

relinquishing without resentment
their weight beneath its power,
how darkness can illumine

what day hid, life hid, to eyes
that grow accustomed to its glare.

STUDIES FOR THE PARLOUR

As the ear is to the orchestration
of sounds near and far, mingling, overlaid,

an orchestra in which the human voice
is an accent as a bird's is, the ring
of cutlery on glass, trowel on brick,

so too the eye,
seeing wallpaper as fabric,
a baby's cheek as millboard,
a butterfly
large and white above a path
that turns out to be a passerby
receding down a lane,

is, to the hierarchies of vision, blind
but by some law of mimetism
able to convey

not only sounds and tastes and smells
but the workings of memory itself,
short-circuiting, choosing what it will

to light on, without a thought
for boundaries, vocabularies
that distinguish the substances
our world and we are made of,
landscape from the flesh.

*

Counting beads, apple pips, tiny things
only we are small enough to count on,

colours by their overlaps
stained, fatigued, in sun-leached lengths
reds no longer red;

turning marbles to the light
and marking indentations, the surface
scratch that tells us where we are
and were before is still the same,

we hold tomorrows solid
in the promise of days to come
when pips give way to orchards –
apple-green, plum-blue, gooseberry-red.

Little do we dream though
that larger minds at ease
with magnitude, expansion,

will be as nonplussed as we are
by the small become dimensionless,
the infinite nonsensical,
by particles as fuzzy

as the kitten in the parlour
collapsing like a star
as it turns to catch its tail.

*

Caught between desire
to enter sitting-rooms illicitly,
standing huge among the ornaments,
chairs we dare not sit on
vacated by the dead,

and the line of least resistance
to rooms we have the run of
among the largenesses of elders
whose bustling is our luxury,
our leave to be ignored in,

we hover on a landing
between the handle and the stairs:

for stowed away with odours, whispers,
mirrors where the souls of those we love
are skyed like chandeliers,

dimensions we know nothing of
– games too human or too pitiable
to let us see with the same eyes
the world we saw this morning –

will lure us in with stories,
feed our hunger for the evidence
of crimes we cannot name.

Sauntering back through doorways then,
with an innocence no sooner lost
than reassumed, we take our place
at table, lift our eyes to faces

knowing nothing of our loss
but betraying, for the first time, theirs.

*

These were rooms
we should not have entered
or entering, not taken fright,
fright at their premonitions,

the story with one ending
we would fight against
and in fighting

corrupt the spirit
that is outside the scope of stories
or is the one that has no end.

*

Behind every keepsake we touch or wonder at
through glass, is a world curtailed,
a household lost to history, a darkened room

where youth betrayed marks time
till it can repossess a body
strewn again with roses,

be claimed again as integral
by the parenthood of death: deaths
that will leave these sitting-rooms
for us to light, too late.

It is now that we want them lit.
Now that we need the dancing. Now
while a rosebud framed in a cream
of skin, black velvet on a neck,

little dreams in its dreams of dancing
of lives lived at such a distance
to those dreams as our dreams now

are to this life lived,
these daisy chains, thumbnail slots,
this small wild life that we ourselves curtailed.

*

Though morning light and evening light
come, like echoes, friable as gunfire

and faith, in a weakening tug-of-war
between the reality that bombards us
and the will to give a body
to the latency inside us, wilts,

the memory of tables
vibrant with refracted light,
objects now forgotten
on their plastics or chenilles,

the child cluttering up the doorway,
the hand that eased her in,

the evocation of a lived-in grace
that continues to sustain us
however gracelessly we live

still connect with a source of love,
that sudden shining space to which words,
conjoining as they near, float in.

*

It was those glass-sprigged afternoons
the best part of us was born in.

Now in a fading light – condensation
rising on the panes, snowing us in –
through a veil of milk

it aches, it glows, it passes . . .

Au Jardin du Luxembourg (detail)
after Henri Cross

If summer had its ghosts, gifts of wind
wind blows to you and whisks away,
then these two small girls

in pale pink flared
like two sweetpeas
I would take for mine and twirl them
to the balustrade . . .

Look how squatting, peering down
they think the ground a river,
a winding in the gravel

whose underwater mysteries
like gaps between our memories
appear and disappear . . .

Like gaps between our memories
that reappear through tow-ropes
seemingly in reach then, far out

where leaves are light
and light is fish
persuade us with a colour,
dissuade us with a depth

twirl them back through leaflitter,
parkland, crossroads, up and over
chimneystacks, birchsmoke, lavender

till, like gaps between our memories,
seed and dust and all wind carries,
they are seen at such a distance

we think them elemental
light, fire, air!

Boy in a Photograph

The wind is up and as we
wind down it grows harder, colder, harsher.
He is the boy

arms around his knees
like a shepherd in a loincloth
dappled under trees

who gazed out to the hills
where life somewhere else raced faster.
His watchface even now

is scudding on his wrist,
tracking like a ninja-cloud
following its master. (The wind

was up but has changed its mind,
only leaves in close-up
are blowing harder . . .)

What was it he was gazing at
across those hills, eyes trained
on a flare, ears keened to a call

that is silent? We have captured him
and blown him up, in shade, in youth,
while his unseen flock

– what flock, what fleece? –
grows larger, smaller, larger.

Coma

Mr Khalvati? Larger than life he was;
too large to die so they wired him up on a bed.
Small as a soul he is on the mountain ledge.

Lids gone thin as a babe's. If it's mist he sees
it's no mist he knows by name. *Can you hear me,
Mr Khalvati?* Larger than life he was

and the death he dies large as the hands that once
drowned mine and the salt of his laugh in the wave.
Small as a soul he is on the mountain ledge.

Can you squeeze my hand? (Ach! Where are the hands
I held in mine to pull me back to the baize?)
Mr Khalvati? Larger than life he was

with these outstretched hands that squeezing squeeze
thin air. Wired he is, tired he is and there,
small as a soul he is on the mountain ledge.

No nudging him out of the nest. No one to help him
fall or fly, there's no coming back to the baize.
Mr Khalvati? Larger than life he was.
Small as a soul he is on the mountain ledge.

Love

When someone sits on your bed
and strokes your hair for a long while
then quietly leaves,

though you feel the mattress
relinquish weight that anchored you
and float unsafe on a surface

that is even but seems to tilt,
though you hear him go, your anchorage
is now less to love than to night and day

whose death and resurrection
you are made
implicit in.

That Night at the Jazz Café

everything about her was beautiful –
skin and hair and eyes proving
clichés holding true.

Was it fluorescence on her cheekbones,
kohl that made her eyes shine, silver
on a thong against her throat

or something in the way she held me
as though no skin or hair or bone
could ever come between us

that made her
– lovely as she'd always been –
that night, so much, much more?

No lover I, to name my love a rose.
No nightingale, old feather-dustered,
grey one I in my daughter's cast-off clothes.

But if I were
I'd wing it to some book-lined aisle
and trapped between two musty shelves

take my feathers to the dust
on weighty tomes; then as paeans rose
from powdery skins, showered in a storm of motes

I too would throw my lot in, give vent
to the songs heard no more in a world
– God keep her safe –

in a world so pleased with its own distaste
what head would lift, librarian stop
for the nightingale and rose?

Apology

Humming your Nocturne on the Circle Line,
unlike the piano, running out of breath

I've been writing you out of my life
my loves (one out, one in).

I've pushed you out of the way to see
what the gaps in my life might look like,

how large they are,
how quickly I could write them in;

and not (at least till I've lost you both)
rewriting you only means

that the spaces I'm not writing in are where
I live.

From *A View of Courtyards*

As though a courtyard were the pedestal
of an airy column roofed in heaven
that as the heavens moved
struck canopies and eaves
with gloom, with gold . . .

as though cornices and lintels,
parapets, architraves etching
shadow steps on terraces, skiagraphs
on brick, were starclocks, sundials,
henges that were homes . . .

the way herdsmen move from slope to slope,
swallows wing from shelf to shelf

at the equinox they moved
lugging bedding, bundles, samovars
across the yard, past the pond
as the season turned
and the weaver's shadow
altered on the loom.

As sunrise spins itself in barberries,
dusk lays its cloth on jams,
so kitchens faced the east
(for morning sun is good sun),
storerooms west and in between,
bicameral as the heart, living room
changed hands.

*

My lover phones to say he's had enough of this
– this never knowing what the time is –
and has bought himself two clocks.

North and south still chiming in my head
the bond between us tightens

and here we are again – though miles apart –
bound in our parallels, as he sets
bells ringing, times
a coincidence of paths.

*

As though an *eyvan*, meeting-point
of greeting and parting, verandah boards
over which a household trudged
or came to rest while an infant slept

were the locus of the soul
between the spirit that is garden,
body that is home

58

(where leg-bindings loosed
even as a journey ended
would let the heart go out,
the soul repair)

undoing damage the old view did
I place myself at thresholds
                        – vernal, autumnal –
garden
where my heart is.

                        *

But when solstice comes I bring
the garden table in, wipe
web and rust, line it up
with a sill whose outer half,
dark in the shade of a rampant vine,
will later catch its raisins.

Seldom use it. Use the stones
of my yard so well they buckle
even more now, tip dangerously
on the top step where my mother fell,
fractured her pelvis – first
in a line of hairline cracks
becoming broken cradles.

Move back in. To my old desk,
an upstairs view of the Archway Road,
next door's rose failing to get a grip
on lace, across the road, my neighbours.

Having lost the power to move at will,
not my own but the seasons',
encumbered with belongings
as though fixtures and fittings
were my metaphor for roots,
I function where my habit is

far from rooms determined
by the gold along a wall,
the alchemy of ponds
turning memory of water
to ice and back to water

and tied to a man
whose contract with mobility
has shunted me off flightpaths,
passed me like a caravan.

*

Lacking southern sun
to leak from an unseen source
behind thicket, cloud or cornstack,
light to make it finite,

my shadow
is all ground on which I walk,
sky to which I turn,
no Mecca, Jerusalem,

no weft or warp
in brickwork or basketry

to say I am, am not, I am.

*

Bedrooms were no battlefields,
no single parents' boxed retreats.
'Don't let the child sleep by herself!'
the women warned as though night
were a stranger offering sweets.

But night was a sling of bedrolls
flung this way, that way, on terraces
or carpets, wherever day had landed
childfalls, summer-calling cousins,
a bridegroom from the city

and bedrooms only latitudes
to give them bed and board
with every night a new – however strange –
configuration, ever redefining
what yesterday found fitting.

As for dining-rooms –
there was no such thing.
A tent perhaps in the orchard
of a house where you spent long summers,
remembered best its boiling vat,
globe of morning milk

or the cooling length of a hallway
where the barest draughts slinked
in and out, reared at the door
as the cloth flared up
and rice came steaming in.

Spines that reached with ease for bread,
even the old, crosslegged,
hipjoints opening down to earth
as though to help her
take them in.

                              *

As though on some dazzling noon verandah
an oil-lamp flame were left, like Cinderella,
still burning in its rags

every year the stars rise later,
emerge in half-light
when one's relation to the half-seen plants,
marrow under giant leaves, seems sacrosanct.

*

In a summer-house of six rooms,
in every room a fireplace, my mother
as a child fitted to their covings
cardboard floors, walls, staircases,

dolls' house interiors she furnished
with matchboxes, wire, felt scraps,
down to tiny rugs that bore, like exports,
the weave of a small girl's hand.

When inhabitants of the real rooms,
curling up on mattresses in moments
before sleep let their eyes fall
on sofas, bureaux, bedroom suites
any western home might have

it must have been as though
falling through a looking-glass
into daughters' lives where fires burn,
wood gleams, bedrooms where in every
nook and cranny is a turning in cocoons,
a learning and unlearning –

the past a cold stone fireplace,
oil-lamp with no wick,
journey into sand . . .

as though a doll's house with no dolls,
dome within a dome, could have prophesied
a shrinking world where the soul mistakes
its yearning for migration
for freedom to cover earth's span

even while furniture is being placed,
carpets tacked and the saw, screw,
unpartnering our seasons, nailing down
the flux, the vagary of maps.

*

As though this loss, giving away
the shirt off one's back, discarding
a love that no longer fits

were only a pupal stage
and this flick of the pink, fireflash,
only fright colouration
before the moth takes wing,

with a click of the latch
I take to the bark,
fly my colours,

survive
on homegrounds wings can match.

*

Ham- is a Persian prefix meaning -mate,
so *hambazi* is a playmate,
hamclassi a classmate
and our word for neighbour
is *hamsayeh*, meaning
one who lives in the same shadow,
a shadow-mate.

A good word
is as a good tree –
its roots set firm,
and its branches in heaven;
giving its fruit at every season
by the leave of its Lord.

I wish to learn the good words
in Qur'an or Bible,
women's words or man's.

I wish to find their offspring,
shadow groupings in the fireplace,
this family or that *fameel,*
madar, pedar, dokhtar.

Learn how to set the future
newly-bathed upon my lap,
bring sky down to wrap us in,
feel myself as human as I am.

Have skylight be to calendar
what soul should be to self

vision
to these small repeated acts.

from Entries on Light

Knocking on the door
    you open, after every
absence – yours or mine –
    as our grounds and elevations
realign themselves, you
    on the step below me, one
or both of the kids above
    I'm struck again as you
face me, turn your back, stricken
    by how small you are.

Bird mother, busy woodland
    creature mother
beginning small and ending small
    I don't believe that it's only
a kernel blown to husk
    the great revolve and vanishing-
point of our figure of eight
    as you cross the kitchen, lower
the gas and we, entering
    let the small shock pass

that is the shock: for
    watching your anxious steps
vanishing deep down corridors
    to return with gifts, it's more
with a sense of vastness, height
    that I see you shrink;
of radiance, like your candle
    lit in the daytime, that I notice
how pale your hair and skin seem
    beside ours.

Dwindling, as hollows
   deepen, brighten and what is
nearest catches light
   in the circle you inhabit and I
inherit, knowing my reach is smaller
   much too small to lift
and shawl you in my arms, fading
   you intensify, like candlelight
on scalloped lace, in the pink
   the very fabric of our lives.

*

Sunday. I woke
   from a raucous night of
seagulls, shafts of sun
   in old bazaars where motes spun

on an abacus for angels.
   Do you long
to go back to that childhood
   the angels asked

in a grown-up body?
   the everlasting blue enquired
as I woke
   to skies washed clean of dust

and churchbells.
   From the acorn of the blind
such seas came
   such tall grave oaks!

Acorn-greys
   of the sea, its pennant rocks
where cormorant wings
   are omens . . . *Do you long*

to go back to that childhood
   the waters asked
in a grown-up body?
   the everlasting shore enquired

with a cockerel
   to wake me in the morning
a dog to guard us
   through the night, one window

pink with sunset, one blue
   with dusk? I could go on and on.
But I am moving into the morning.
   I am making do with light.

                *

Today's grey light
   is of
light withheld but
   softly
shyly like a sheltered
   girl's.

It's a
   light in gentle
motion
   like a young girl
sitting
   splaying her skirts

her listening smiles
   around her.
When
   barefoot
she disappears
   momentarily to another

sky
   gleams like glassware
we can hear not see
   we
contract but air
   expands

into a memory
   she has thrown
behind her.
   And in the memory is
light
   and lightness.

*

Scales are evenly
   weighed, inside
outside. Light is
   evenly poised
– blur to the gold
   glare to the blue –
it's twilight.
   In two minds.

Who can read by
   a lamp, focus
land's outline?
   But blue soon
sinks and gold
   rises. Who
can stay the balance
   if light can't?

*

Streetlamps
   threw battlements of
shadow on a lawn, somewhere
   a travelling

clock ticked; rockplants
   hung faceted
with lurid
   orange raindrops

dustbin lids
   gleamed
under gutter-pipes
   and eaves.

But given
   the minerality of
shorelife, rain's afterlife
   it seemed

with a moon in the sky
   tide going out – and
wave coming in on wave –
   a miracle

that the one should draw
   the other, as though
gravity were more to do
   with weightlessness than weight.

*

The heavier, fuller, breast
     and body grow, the higher
flies the thought, the more
     rarefied its air.

It is the law of action:
     the stronger a gesture, the lighter
its recovery. On a black sea
     how far the spirit sails!

                    *

Through me light drives
     on seawall, fencepost, brittle
spears of lavender. A light
     at its most inexplicable.
In reversals, shadows, replications
     of a ceiling light, table lamp

amber stars that now signal
     now don't, across water.
A world turned back-to-front
     where natural arbiters
of light, sea and sky
     are silenced. Light on

passers-by, dimpled on the gloss
     of windowsills and who knows
if foliage shadowed on stone
     is from creeper or curtain?
Even our image in glass, like knowledge
     forgotten, startles us. How bright

the lamp is in the garden!
    Between this world and the next
runs a white rail to impede
    our fall, illuminate
our light-world's edge, the selvage
    of our small front gardens.

                    *

In the amber
    are the leather globe, quillpen;
bald velvet, Red
    Admirals, in the amber are their leaded

lines, candle weeping at the window
    a husband's shirt hung up
to dry, a crib
    and a child's turned head.

In the amber is the smell of
    fox, rosin, stale
tobacco, in the amber is the hallowed glow
    of something old, and male.

                    *

The air is the hide
    of a white bull, the light
as tame. But if a storm brews
    this afternoon
when bladderwrack will be
    black at his hooves
and the first white waves
    lather him up into seafoam

she will mount him, rein him
in with the right horn
and as shorelights fade
riding oblivion back into time
where the light of the rosehip
founders, see
tameness
reveal its astonishing face.

*

I'm silenced in.
Bowled over. No
globe so round, star
as silver, though I've
seen a thousand
suns, ever rose
like this, a sun
of grapefruit silver.

Ghostliest of
beginnings:
a nocturne in the morning
a Shangri-La
in the upper pane, turn off
the light, let
acid glow
from every angle.

One empty room
can't see it, walk down
the street you'll never
catch it, even the skylights'
gold denies
a white eye holed
into the mind of heaven.
For a moment I was

threatened. Depend on it
   the sun, the moon
depend on him
   who loves you, even
the moon can rise in the morning
   Shangri-La come to town
the beautiful
   be terror.

*

I hear myself in the loudness
   of overbearing waves, you
in the soft retreat, if-and-but
   of defeated sighs, the tug
that gets me nowhere.
   It'll never end. Sound
of the sea – still Sappho's sea –
   the yes-and-no of lovers.

Inland, I dreamt of hearing
   waves again but here
sea in my ears, watching reds
   of life-jackets, blues
of a hull and sails, recapture
   in the yes-and-no of my own blood
only the to-and-fro of our endless
   drift – my bed a beach, you said.

Everything I ever said about you
   was true; but trueness
in that tone and at that pitch
   never helps. How could we help
having loved elsewhere too much
   and I don't mean other lovers
but homelands, other cultures
   pulling oceans in their wake?

*

Speak to me as shadows do
    where light comes through
perforations of snow-white lace

attenuating on a surface
    eyelets into ovals
softening prisms into flakes.

Speak to me as echoes do
    attenuating, softening
the thing first harshly said.

*

This book is a seagull whose wings
    you hold, reading journeys between
its feathers. It flutters, dazzles.
    Sings cleanly in shade. Sharpens
your ears to journeys life's taken
    that scraping of a mudguard, tinkling
of stays. Its spine has halved the sun.
    Sun fired it with a nimbus.
A wheelchair passes, crunching on shingle.
    This book, set off by wind, makes you
long for the world, to take lungfuls
    of pleasure, save scraps on quick raids.
So that sated, you turn, blot out the world
    enter another, settle for words.

*

I'm opening
   the door of shadow
on a page. In the doorway
   stands a poem

like a girl in a dress.
   I see through her
to her feelings –
   absent on the page, absent

as a house might be
   through an overgrowth
of ivy – his
   heart, his despair.

She wants him
   not to talk of
leaves, nor to stand
   in sunlight.

To close the door
   on strangers, lie on her
as a sunlit page
   might close on grey.

Not a sheet
   between them, not even
the gap where a thumb
   disengaged.

*

One upper pane by a windchime
   her moon shines through;
plants, tall or hanging, are
   reminiscent of tunnelled trees
while a fern at eye-level
   confirms some forest floor.

Out there a dog barks rapturously;
    nearer home her cat, whose kittens
died in the litter, scrabbles earth
    with nonchalance, jet streaming
down her coat. How does one invade
    people's spaces with such ease

or people's bodies for that matter
    and is this bad or good?
As natural a brutality as is
    natural to commingle
breath, moisture, soil and seed
    in the underbrush of woods?

                    *

I've never been in a hurry
    to find you out, letting
you pledge yourself
    to the oracular. Once

I might have been
    a cabin in the woods
a patch of grass where you studied
    Latin verbs with a friend

who studied you
    so you began to have a sense
of friendship and with it
    loneliness.

I came to you
    through a woman once
who missed me with you around
    and wanted the three of us

to make space and time
    for a taste
of my vernacular. Now
    with my name on your lips

and hers wiped off, she thinks:
    I thought you weren't
interested – you said you weren't –
    in *happiness*.

*

It's all very well
    for me you think and I
for trees and sky and wind;
    blind to the grief
beyond our walls, who can tell
    what shadow falls, or leaf?

*

Show, show me.
    But you see
only through the lens
    of your own eye. Light
strikes your bed
    differently
towerblocks I like to see in a
    cityscape at night
loose screams you hear
    differently – such
fortresses we are.
    Show, show me.

Let the blind lead the blind?
    But we're not. We see
a burnstripe on an arm
    we may or may not recognise
utopias emitting light
    that strikes differently
or fails to light.
    Not isolation
but the singularity of thought
    – thought that freeze-frames
feelings
    we might have had in common –

is the fortress that I plead from
    and am heard
bell-like
    in the service of your own life
lovingly and with empathy
    but when it comes to mine
how should I
    have the heart to tell you, *show* you
that it's not the scream
    in my throat, nor the thought
in my head, nor the light of beliefs
    I steer by?

                    *

: that sky and light and colour
    cloud, clearings

should raise me, strip me down
    to the bare bones

of vocabulary: rise fall sea sky
    a tree and not a sycamore

flower and not a bluebell
   till the agony of daily life

falls away, like ground from a tilting
   plane, drops far below me.

*

I love all things in miniature
   – the blue tree whose sprigs
are like the lilac's in miniature –
   and small things too since they
recollect a child's eye view
   of a small world inside a large
in which small things might represent
   the large – acorn cup a cup, sprig
a tree – and because miniatures are
   fully-formed and in completion
futureless, as if childhood itself
   were arrested, made redeemable.

Lying belly down on grass, level
   with a sparrow's eye as it cocks
its head, engages without seeing us
   I remember how our first lessons
were tailored to a scale in which
   the child loomed large, creatures
small and therefore it was incumbent
   on our stature to feel tenderness.
I felt it for a moment and have lost it
   now that the mind has taken flight
left a birdless stretch of grass
   so much larger than itself.

*

In that childhood time
        of peering out
from a hut of leaves
        at the ebb and flow –

though little did
        sun perhaps on a glint
of straw, wind
        ballooning a shirt or branch –

each gust and pause, drift
        of skin between
warm and cold, was a source
        of mindless patience.

How a world could be
        changed from moment
to moment, broken
        by sudden entrances

a bumblebee, helicopter;
        resumed and our
solitude, brushing wings
        with its passing by

be, for the contact
        safer: this
was the ebb and flow
        we watched for

as though each shift of
        grass, flight of paper
float of shadow across a path
        weren't just earth's

response to a moving heaven
        but the heart's reply
shaping life
        and we its recording angel.

*

Light's taking a bath tonight
    in the sea's enamelled
blue-rimmed bath, lying along
    its length. Hair submerged
thighs and belly in mile-long
    strips showing through white
between limbs and fingers
    bluer depths.

Light's closing her eyes
    not once but twice – once
face up, once facing down
    from her ceiling mirror.
In rising steam, the longest
    bath earth's ever seen, closing
her lids on sea and sky till only
    mist and vapour stir.

                        *

Dawn paves its own way
    if what we mean by dawn
is sunrise. The sky's already
    light by the time the sun
comes up, rising on its own
    prediction of the day.
This is how art is made.
    And memory. And love.

First, the halo overhead.
    Next, the body. Last
the roots like the final
    rays of the sun spiralling
as earth pulls free of them
    and they of earth. Then
illumination's width and frame.
    This is how love is made

rising into a desire
    for love, however grey
the outlook, late the hour
    hard for faith and fear
to pave the way. Love
    full-face. Preordained
as sunrise, chasing after
    the ghost of its own grace.

*

With finest needles
    finest beads
lawn and dew are making
    a tapestry of water . . .

*

When sky paints itself
    with daubs and puffs of
cloud-sponge, wrinkles
    the silk surface of the sea, trails
fingers of light on a misted
    ground to illuminate
its manuscript
    what should I do
but put down my pen, marvel
    at its changes before the marvellous
puts away its own pen and
    the sun, so small, so glorious
rising in a cone of light, sinks
    behind the grey again, leaving
a scar of rosy fire in melting pinks
    and vanishes?

*

There's no jewel
   we can think of
that's orange. But she
   has studded her hair
with clips and stars
   trailed from her fingers
chains and ropes
   hung from her throat
twin pendants
   in cleavages of water

flung anklets, bracelets
   to bob on circling floats.
She's scattered a fistful
   of uncut gems
over shore and hill, a chip or two
   dropped on a skyline boat;
set five ablaze
   in a row of lamps and saved
for her royal knuckle
   the brightest stone.

But we who pass by railings
   facelessly in twos
past necklaces of traffic
   glass cases banked with jewels
will have to choose
   from local
topaz, tourmaline, citrine
   quartz for there's no
jewel we can think of
   that's orange.

*

Moons come in all the colours
   of the rainbow. Combine them
too. I wish I could see such moons
   parade themselves night after night
across my window. I wish I could
   keep awake to watch such moons.

And if I could, I'd wish words were
   inks, inks quills for lyres, wish
I could play and sing along with the words
   like Sappho. I'd stand at the window
stripped, take colour from the moon
   as it shone through cloud, marbled me

head to toe, in rainbow. I'd learn
   like Uri Geller, eyes closed, palm
on my belly, moon on my hand, to read
   colour through touch, open my eyes
to have the moon confirm, at a stroke
   the shades we'd been through.

Perhaps I could keep these colours
   under my skin, transmit them
the way you say my eyes change colour
   when we're making love, through
my entire length lying under you
   to your every pore. Then you'd know

know in your bones how to read me
   how to match my moods.
That'd be good. Better than clues
   most men I know are blind to.
Most men are colour-blind did you know?
   when it comes to grey & green & blue.

*

Why not mention the purple flower
    token of exchange
between this world and the next?
    Ignore the wind

and the wild wet light blossoming
    as the purple does
when you draw the curtain to inspect
    the light but your eye rebounds

from a flower, colour
    you can't quite name.
Purple will do. What does the shade
    under grey stone walls

grey underside of wings you saw
    when the sun blazed
turn blue, cornflower blue as gulls flew
    into the face of the sun

in another lightning exchange, matter?
    Mention the purple, stay close
to the heart: remember
    when the curtain is drawn

on the infinite blue that today
    is infinite grey
it's the heart that knows
    the best in its gift

to exchange for the gift of sky and light
    and though you can't place
its name or shade or hearing
    the cynic's groan at the mere

mention of flowers – oh not again –
    retreat like a snail in your shell
throw shame to the winds, gravitas to the skies
    and do it! – mention the purple.

*

One sky is a canvas for jets and
    vapour trails, one
Venetian. One a dawn that may spoil
    or bloom, the other
a perfection. On towerblocks or grand
    canals, roundabouts or
basins. Removal trucks, motorbikes
    icecream vans are gilded
in the one, in the other, silence is golden.
    On a moat in Dresden
there are swans, colonnades in water.
    In the Piazetta everyone
is dressed in white, everything is
    lined with copper.

Some will look for immanence
    in a shadow on the wall sinking
through water, or focus where the shadow ends
    on a bricked diagonal of gold
and remember how sun warms brick and linen
    in offices and houses
how glory that was general
    is particular to them.
One is the glory of the yet-to-be, one
    of a past that reminds us
how we've seen it in our own lives exactly
    as it used to be but were
blinded by those lives, distracted from our own
    perfections.

*

Black fruit is sweet, white is sweeter.
   Sweeter than any white grape, white fig
is white mulberry, too sweet to eat
   without water.

And water, catching casts of berry
   is bluer in its blue-washed pool
than any sky in living memory, boasting
   hot summers in England.

If England is small
   this corner of heaven
is smaller. Barely two bow-lengths
   but morning as long

as the Garden on the Day of Rising
   and evening the length
of a life so little wasted, little room
   has been left for regret.

Instead there is shade and silence.
   One as deep as the other.
Yet for all their depth, buoyant
   as a salt sea, more buoyant for the scent

of jasmine from four corners; only
   tuberose clutches more at the heart
when the heart's at home but home's
   where the heart grows greyer.

So if I were tell you in future
   how sweet were the berries
left lying in a bowl
   dried and greyed and inedible

once sweet enough to bring tears
   to your eyes, I swear to God
not a word would ring true, for even truth
   lies in the face of the incomparable.

*

He's tying up the gypsophila
   that lay like a snowspray
on his emerald grass. Dark emerald
   that reminds me of Rilke's
dark evergreen, *our hours of pain.*
   And has flung a bouquet

of dead daisies there. Uprooted
   like aftersmells of love they remind me
of Valentine's smell, *corn and milk*
   coming through her tears.
Are those deadheads still on the pavement
   in that backstreet I think

is Tehran? The walled tree's
   whose mock-stars fall
out of its skirts to a shade
   the width of a smell: a white cocoon
I can enter, stoop in, bow my head
   to a guttering star, bridal-veiled.

                      *

And had we ever lived
   in my country
you might have asked
   had I returned

were backstreets cool
   in siesta heat
did hawkers call
   the mulberry thrive

on neglect?
   Who can I ask
of mulberry and mint
   courtyard shade

so alive with presence
    when no one's around
but a burning sun
    and grapes, walled-in?

Who can I ask
    to ensure a return
have me to stay, receive
    my gifts?

                    *

Winter's strains
    have surfaced to skin
under bra-strap, thigh elastic
    stone under skull and towel.

As wind blows, sun burns
    I turn to the ground's pull
record in every crease, every
    three-ringed knuckle

the ferocity of white.
    Tonight, against your knees
two shields of red when I
    near you, flashing moon-teeth

to your laughter, blackberry
    nipples to your lips
the nightsky we see by will see us
    by our eyes and teeth, like lamps

cut out on its own black skin
    sickle moons on winter
nights when we, worm-pale, sleep
    in rooms as black as ink.

                    *

And in the sea's blackness sank
    wreckage of the day
its faces, voices, stops and starts
    while to the surface rose
lights, lapping of waves
    squawks of invisible birds
we heard as apertures
    in a low dark sky –
the glittering crust that to an eye
    seeing for the first time
evidence of man's night on earth
    might be as intricate, luminous
as space to ours and wondrous
    in its buoyancy, littoral
between depths and heights, electric
    on its charts of glass
as peace might be
    putting out without sound or sail.

*

When space is at its emptiest
    an undervoice in which
songs of the sea, lamp, grass
    inside one's orbit sing

then space assumes a radiance
    an open throat through which
songs of the sea, lamp, grass
    sing not of themselves but of

something old, something new
    something borrowed, something blue
something, whoever it belongs to
    in which other lives begin.

*

Was it morning, night?
   I remember
only because I have it
   now – stamped when a baby
was born in those days –
   her footprint.

Blue-inked, small enough
   to fit a notepad
like the first
   inkling of a poem.
What time was it?
   I remember

winter light on that
   boulevard, some park
the Shah had planted
   opposite, how poor it looked
how poor the strollers
   were in their shabby coats

mountain light and rows
   of saplings.
If she asks again
   her time of birth, I'll give her
mountain light and her own
   loveliness, I'll even

give her the name
   of a boulevard, hospital . . .
Apadana . . . Pars . . . everything
   but the amnesia
before
   that footprint.

*

Curling her tail
    and staring
not quite sure who
    I was
how many kittens
    I too
had had, stalking
    past as
disdainfully
    as blackness
smallness
    warrants, this
is what she
    left me with:
curvature
    and silence.

                    *

His 18th. He likes Chinese.
    Café Rouge'll do. I've spent
a fortune on his lamp, lamp to light
    his future, throw light on him.

I see it on a piano, YAMAHA in gold
    torso in shadow, right hand
with his father's fingers no his own
    plying up and down up and down

though only over a small stretch
    the way it used to drive me mad
make me tear my hair, get rid of him.
    A lamp to light him. Something

to keep forever we both agreed.
   The way my mother's mother
scarved and sunglassed in the sky
   would want it. No pyrotechnics.

While the fireworks in his body
   are what he himself once called
in between the keys. When I first read that –
   of a restaurant he'd have for jazz

he wrote, called *In Between The Keys* –
   something flashed inside me. Like
scattered light, his mother's skirts
   inside him. I dream of him

four years old, abandoned in a bath
   the tears on him. Squib, damp squib.
I taste the salt, his lashes' salt.
   My fingerling. My waterlips.

*

Staring up from his pram to the sky
   through mobile leaves that so
transfixed him, no matter who smiled
   and cooed, whose head might suddenly
block his light, those sea-washed eyes
   that had never yet seen sea
wouldn't flinch, barely blinked
   and when at last they panned from
tree to you, it would seem as if
   time itself had been scanned
so slowly did sight catch up with vision
   vision give way to a human hold.

And though he'd sit for hours, tearless
    and wide awake, you'd lift him
shoulder him with kisses, words, any
    bauble waved like a flag to bring it
home to him, him home to you.
    But even his eyelashes, so long
and straight, channelled his gaze
    outwards and onwards and irises
so light, so green, implied nothing
    but light behind them, as if his mind
had fled to the back of his skull
    and bled every shadowy lobe.

As you carried him in to a sunless
    hall, behind your back, were
those eyes trained down on a lane
    where the pram still stood?
A white sheet rumpled, an awning
    of leaves shadowed on sheet
and hood. As you shifted his weight
    and revolved to the door
between him and the light, did something
    pass – like a tryst, deferred
drawn up through those eyes to a sky
    he was saying goodbye to?

                        *

New Year's Eve.
    Under a sky as high as this
we are cut-glass, space-lattices
    for broken narratives, like
mountain cities left behind
    through the mind's eye revisited.

Pavement weeds are faint with light.
  Birds raucous in the bushes.
Perspectives in the High Street
  lowered, lengthened, acquire
the clarity of paintings. Glass
  animals of childhood, horses

seals balancing on crystal globes
  are as we are to the sky
whose distance finds no measure
  between cloud and cloud, this year
and the next, being the same high blue
  we saw when we were small

and our menagerie of bright revolves
  already broken narratives.
Against the unbroken blue, nothing
  is not nervous, alive with light:
stream, swans, bicycles, elude our need
  to follow one train of thought

of wing or water, adjacent roofs
  throwing down a flock of birds
like a gauntlet to the wind, stand
  impassive as it lifts, whirls
on a clap of laughter . . . and as we
  on foot, happy to be human, move on.

                    *

In this
  country
the brilliance of
  sun on snow
is as though
  not love
but belief in love
  laid its hand on you

you the adolescent
   whose world was always
gilded, warmed
   even on its highest
snows
   and now
every berried branch
   you look up and through

slopes
   of builders' sand
remind you of last year
   when it laid its
hand on you
   gentle
as the turning of a
   calendar.

*

Here's dusk to burrow in;
   doorstep light where children
going home from school, mothers
   at the open doors of cars
forms having lost their shadows
   when the sun went down

become them. Trailing to peer
   dim-sightedly at a glove on a spike
creature or leaf curled on stone
   coin or charm in the rubble
as if, too late, they were looking
   to learn a landscape they know

wind will shift, night remove
   they freeze, sniff air –
freedom just yards from the warren.
   But thresholds braved today
as tomorrow's beckon, will darken.
   So catch, in the last of the light

the last child, mitten and scarf
   ankle and calf from kerb to car
the snowberry-white last gesture
   for that tail-end of our darkening
forms – *entre chien et loup* – that
   mark and its marked erasure

is the theft and gift, fang and fur
   of dusk, this double vision:
a sighting of metamorphic laws only
   dusk affords with menace and grace
but eyes inscribe, mistakenly
   as last transitions.

*

All yellow has gone from the day.
   I'm left with the blues and greys.

Pool of light on the desk.
   Strangely content. Perhaps

night is more my element.
   How white white flowers seem

skin showered, oiled, and the day
   but a night away. The days ahead . . .

*

While the tulip threatens
     to lose one leaf
and a pigeon
     perched on a tile-red roof

grooms another, ruff
     to the light
articulating
     iridescence on its purple patch;

while a small girl plays
     with her football in a coat
as red as tulips
     and my son now smiles at children

being a man;
     as days pass, post comes and goes
without news, across
     empty lots, back gardens

as far as
     waterways to mill towns
these urban tracts between us
     spread

as if they
     could be our river now
and these desks where we ply
     a trade, riverbanks.

*

Darling, your message on the phone
    made me cry. I phoned you back
to let you hear the tears
    in my voice but your phone
was engaged. On second thoughts
    I'll write you this with
tears gone from my eyes and cloud
    like smoke from smokestacks
moving across a lining of blue
    that is our sky, that no matter
how clouds cross, yes, my smoke rises
    – I'm not smoking now –
we've always known lies behind them
    as the heart and breath behind
your vowels – such a long ah
    in darling! – as tears behind these
words, not sad tears nor tears
    to lay on you but dried tears to
'open the eyes of the heart'
    as they say back home – and this is
back home – to beginnings we always
    dreamed of, now lay a claim to
not knowing if dreams come true.
    I'd thank you but *'it hasn't a thankyou'*
and I haven't words large and clean
    enough – the phone's ringing now . . .
it wasn't you . . . and this sentence
    if I go on like this is never
going to end as you aren't with me
    nor I with you. I wish I could slice
that bit of the tape and keep it forever
    but neither you nor I know how to.

*

Is it before or after the fiesta?
   Have the revellers gone in
that the sunflower leans
   like a bystander in shade;
with the bowl of the fountain
   empty, holding last night's
laughter, is the wedding, fiesta
   today? Who are the bride
and groom, sea and sun, heat
   and flesh, in a sprinkler's
arc, are the bridesmaids sparrows
   seen through spray? Why
does an air of expectation meet
   before its joy, regret?

                    *

On a late summer's day that draws
   to a close as summer does
– one closing within another –
   I remember tree peonies

deep in shade, globe within globe
   wearing colours on their sleeves
like doublets slashed with crimson
   and regretting how flowers

so gorgeous, luxurious, seemed
   destined to a half-life, even
in their prime only ever
   half-open. Not my kind of flower

I'd half a mind to say.
   Now summer rises, rises
then droops its head. The stem
   of the sky's too weak for sun

lolling its face in shade.
   Summer's a slipped
umbrella, the melancholy
   when everything's been said.

                    *

102

First you invite me to tea under your apple tree and now
    send me a photograph of where we sat, you, still ill
by your herbs in shade and I in a wedge of sun angled
    under apples. Let me not break the chain. Send you
a poem of your photo of the patio of your new home, wish you
    entirely better. The doorway's as narrow in its light
as shadow's broad and black in the kitchen. Blackest of all
    your bike in silhouette. And the apple tree just visible
where bright light grows on a shrub I'd know, if it weren't
    for those clumps of flowering light you knew I'd like
has no flowers. But what can I write that's not in the eye?
    How something tall and narrow can suggest a yardage of sun
an L, one arm of which you'll plant, where drainpipes ask for disguise
    with shade-lovers? How, in a city's heart, Elephant & Castle
you can be in the heart of the country, how knee-high trellises
    fronting allotments whose tenants stop to talk to you, spell
an other worldliness? But you know all that. How memory
    speaks to the image, image to the word. How inadequate
we are in our borrowings, not knowing if by saying *I'm like you*
    we do violence. Thank you for the herbs, tea, the photo.
Think of this as a postcard but more than that, a short time
    spent in your company, after the event, a recognition of those
differences we run into now and then, alternatives we never chose –
    patios with loaded apple trees, herb troughs, neighbouring
histories of architects and saints in the churches of south London;
    other people's knowledge vaguely interesting, vaguely boring
lifestyles, lovelives and sometimes even illnesses worn transparent
    on a face that brings it home: the equity no one has in common;
differences that now and then make us feel are of less account
    than an hour or two – and I hate that word affirming but –
affirming, the way women do when we say *me too*, each other.
    (And the facings of your bookshelves like an opening accordion.)

*

Everywhere you see her, who could have been
    Monet's woman with a parasol
who's no woman at all but an excuse for wind –
    passage of light-and-shade we know
wind by – just as his pond was no pond
    but a globe at his feet turning to show
how the liquid, dry, go topsy-turvy, how far
    sky goes down in water. Like iris, agapanthus
waterplants from margins where, tethered
    by their cloudy roots, clouds grow underwater
and lily-floes, like landing-craft, hover
    waiting for departure, she comes at a slant
to crosswinds, currents, against shoals of sunlight
    set adrift, loans you her reflection.
I saw her the other day I don't know where
    at a tangent to some evening, to a sadness
she never shares. She wavers, like recognition.
    Something of yours goes through her, something
of hers escapes. To hillbrows, meadows
    where green jumps into her skirt, hatbrim shadows
blind her. To coast, wind at her heels, on diagonals
    as the minute hand on the hour, the hour
on the wheel of sunshades. Everywhere you see her.
    On beaches, bramble paths, terraces of Edwardian
hotels. In antique shops, running her thumb along
    napworn velvet. A nail buffer. An owl brooch
with two black eyes of onyx. Eyes she fingers.
    But usually on a slope. Coming your way.

*

Don't draw back
    his lilac said.
Don't pin me down
    his blue and grey.
Whose tears are pricking
    eyelids? asked his pink
on snow. Mine, black answered
    mine that light can't shed.

*

Light comes between us and our grief
    flushes it out with gold.
And when skies are overcast, still
    we collude with clouds, building
grey to a spur for light that will
    drive us to stand at a distance
from ourselves, small at the barricades
    clouds burst to let grief go.
Light leaves us bereft in one sense
    only to flood us with sensation
bleeding out grief in a bright dissolve.
    There's something I can't hold
in the presence of light, great light, or feel
    as a river might feel for its stones.

*

Why does the aspen tremble
  without a trace of wind?
Under its spire, close
  your eyes, listen.
Listen to Khadijah. Her
  big heart beating.
He is bringing a new wife
  home today. Half her age.
Twice her beauty. Aisha, Aisha.
  Listen to the leaves.
What the Bosnian Moslem women say.
  The story they weave.

Khadijah is not jealous.
  Under the awning she
stands, arms folded.
  Arms she will open wide.
Large, generous Khadijah
  ample-limbed . . .
But when a horse
  pricks up its ears, backs
two paces, whinnies, a current
  faint as the morning star
runs through her, air around her
  ripples, stills.

Like an arrow loosed from
  a quiver, that impulse
shot from her heart
  is caught in the arms
of aspen, sends a shiver
  through every leaf.
And thereafter, though there are
  no aspens in Arabia
though there is
  no wind, this is why
the aspen trembles
  over the bed's thin stream.

*

Boys have been throwing
    stones all day; even
the youngest – barely two –
    could throw stones that reached

the water. Years ago
    you threw them too from a beach
or bank and I, whose throws
    even dogs disdain, valiantly tried

to skim them.
    I read in Sylvia's diary
of stones the colour of fox – and so they are
    from a distance.

Apricot stones, filters.
    I bury them under a red-fox coat
of shingle. Camouflage
    so much of the past in my rush

to near the future. Far away as ever.
    Whatever the shore, wherever
the blue, letters locked in drawers
    rowboats, wells

in dogeared snapshots, postcards sent
    but mysteriously
repossessed years later –
    hidden pockets of a globe

we once called home
    are still at home and will
when I least expect, resurface
    in the gap between

boy and girl, whose stones soar
    and sink without trace
or land, marked
    'return to sender'.

*

107

Foreshortened
  light claws out of the sea
skin-puckered. Reluctant
  to leave the great outdoors
– benchwood warm –
  huddles behind grey towels.
Light's eyes are blurry with
  salt, heels white with water.

Fists knuckled and locked
  against his mouth, scanning
a roughening shore, he squints, wavers . . .
  Makes to go then, dropping
his towels, shoulder-blades twin
  shafts of sun, he's back in the swim
to brave out the day as
  yours lengthens.

*

On a diving-board, against
  a centrefold of sky they queued:
eyes rheumy, hair plastered, scars
  whitening under welts of pus
and queue there still as if
  in the after-image, sparkling off
into scythes of light, were the gold
  and ground of every plunging replay.

Knowing replay is not countless
  that water and its breaking
close on a lap behind them
  was it for this that they
showed no mercy, shrieking, shoving
  the weakest from the highest board
clowning about with variants
  on the perfect fall from grace?

Wanting nothing less than a commandment
    for themselves to hurl, shatter, resurface
into their features, for this they held
    nose and breath, plummeting faster
than the speed of sight, fell and kept on
    falling until, in that last recall
higher than the highest board, they froze
    in that blue inhuman air?

*

I have removed the scaffolding
    from the Parthenon. In the city
of the mind's eye, acropolis of
    dawn, now scaffold it with rays.

I have turned its north face to face
    east, ramparts into London smog
and where blue begins its columns rise
    where blue is clear, they end.

As for height, I have left it where
    it was, dwarfed in the eyes of Gods
at whose feet my chimney pots are
    fat, terracotta statuettes.

In place of white Pentelic marble, I summon
    time as a counterweight. Time
in the guise of sun too high for rays.
    And imagination too slow to keep pace.

Summon them in the name of lightness
    for by their own dead weight
they make our images so weightless
    that even in this short span, despite

millennia stone survives, this
    atonement, my monument to memory
has gone up in smoke, left nothing
    but a few clouds to bar its trace.

*

So high up in a house
    being alone is ethereal
like a wind curled up on its ankles
    precarious in a tree

or lung-stain of a shadow
    in a corner of an attic
you can't inhabit as every breath
    must leave its branch

hoarsely clamber down
    to converse with what is real.
So why delay? Is being alone
    the greater love, the greater loss

the ineffable, unreal: touch
    of a cold cheek rosy
in a lower room too much
    the open sore that never bleeds?

*

These homes in poems –
    how large they were. Upwards
and sideways. How they housed
    in sun and gloom, those loved
unloving fathers' ghosts
    mothers medicinal as scents
that drifted in from trees
    with unusual names.

These homes had attics, tea-chests.
    Country or cathedral views
woodsmoke like epitaphs
    scrawled indelibly on air.
Air was always resident.
    Charged with the many duties
loss imposes on a habitation
    whose owners are elsewhere.

(Air must don its apron, dust
    shafts of light, shake out
camphor and cobweb, breathe
    rings on the bell.)   Above all
there was singing. As if the mind
    had climbed to its highest
landing, from an upstairs room
    someone's voice.

And the house rose only
    that this voice should be
embodied, bulwarked against
    wind by walls, rooted
in nursery furniture, friendships
    only flyleaves know
married to its elements, skeleton
    and soul and carried downstairs.

For those who have no homes like
    these, no fork in the road to mark
their winding route from others'
    let the house that the song sings
into being serve as a stopping-inn
    to share a couch, pass the jug
re-sing the song that will carry
    over wilderness and mountain.

                    *

For you, who are
    a large man, a large
man and a delicate poet, whose
    flagstoned hall I have
stood on the brink of, ice-
    blue walls been warmed in

and learned, looking at your
    wife, your beautiful
wife – and you think so too –
    how warm ice-blue can be
like an aureole for eyes
    of blue, Nordic hair of honey

and slept in white and blue
    on an empty floor
at the top of your house
    padded in socks on carpet
to a bathroom through books
    and books you have lived through

and that living-through I catch
   a glimpse of, too awed
to envy, empties me till I am only
   filled with a sense of books
unread, life unlived, a span
   of time and space out there

much too late for the taking
   but not for lifting
as I did the patchwork quilt
   of blue on white, a corner of . . .
for you, I felt like writing
   a line, out of the blue, a poem.

*

When
   against a cloth
of blue
   silver linings are
reversed
   then, unfrocked
like a single
   diamond drop
vested head to toe
   in blinding white
light enters
   as *Der Rosenkavalier*.

*

The gate has
    five bars and five
bars of song
    for whatever reason I might
want to sing
    as I climb the stile to a
solitude
    escaping from itself
in smoke-filled rooms
    would be more than enough
to swing me
    as the river does
white heifer on the hill
    from the
dark side of solitude
    to its light-starved
underside
    silver-fir green.

                    *

I'm reading with the light on
    though it's 4 o'clock in the afternoon
and the skylight overhead, masked
    with a calico blind, casts
a whiteness in the air as if a blanket
    of snow had covered the pane
and light was filtering through flakes.
    Outside, the freshness, suspense

of after-rain. So the reading-lamp
    behind my shoulder, casting
a small gold glow, is relegated
    by natural light to illumination
that only alters colour. But since
    I'm reading poetry, that small gold glow
having little to do with visibility and
    from a source outside my vision, seems

to have taken upon itself the task
of a farmstead light at the end of a path
when you first emerge from a forest –
light that the poem heads towards
or has come from, light you don't read
lines by but between them by, warming
as the page descends. And when the page
is turned, the glow recedes so that

lamplight, skylight, gold and snow
merge and the first words you read
The dandelion does not yet blossom here
pull you back to their own
gold, light, snow, sky, up on to a ridge
– the old road between farmsteads? –
leaving the poem out in the open
and the forest on the page.

*

Times are – thinking about new wine
in old bottles – when the mind
flooded with sensations only
the old words make sense of, tastes
as if never before, their delicacy
of invention, proof of the pudding.
Such a dawn was this: of promise
and illusion, birds' proverbial choruses.

I mourn the untold usages still
redolent of grape, of yeast, if I had
new eyes, ears for the daily round
they sprang from, mediations
between man, nature, beast, little altered
in a world as young as ours – evil
being no sign of age, corruption
no condition of maturing.

I mourn their number
   and their ease. Reading
won't bring them back. Rather
   drive them further back to the cask
the cave they were laid down in –
   the mouth and mind that framed them
mouth and mind that now
   consign them to the bin.

Unless, that is, we read the world
   that informed them with the same
immediacy we assume when we read
   or word our own and by doing so
find how the same words fit.
   John, at dawn today I read your book
– as I wrote you and I'll write it twice –
   caught between two sleeps.

*

Like old red gold welded
   by rhythm where the words
have cracked
   snatches of a poem
set behind my back, keep setting
   as the sun does.

I recite them
   not by memory, by heart.
The rooms of memory
   are dark. Rooms of the heart
flared with dreams where
   blur-faced as white pansies

children lining windows
   thumb their nose
at memory, go
   fishing about in the bloodstream
for slips of the tongue
   figures of speech, puns

that work both day and night.
   Work
and then run out.
   What heart knows is battered
molten, eroded, with nothing to cling to
   but love. Memory's

a bad mother, neither oral
   nor literate.
Heart has her number
   holds her to
her smell, bare bones
   the heart's refrain like rock.

                    *

An Iranian professor I know asked me
   the first time we met, as he'd asked so many
students: *Saheb-del* – how would you say in English
   Saheb-del, can you translate it? And each time
he pronounced the words his fingers tolled the air
   like a bell, a benediction. Years have passed.

Saheb means master, owner, companion; *del*
   means heart. Heart's companion, keeper?
Heart's host? And in those years I've asked
   friends who in turn have asked friends
who know Urdu, Farsi, and no one has come up with
   the English for *Saheb-del*. Is it a name

117

for the very thing that won't translate? And why
   don't I remember having heard it said?
They say it of people who are hospitable, 'godly',
   I'd say it of the professor himself. Trust him
to keep asking, us to keep failing, and if we can't recall
   its tone, tenor, with what word shall we keep faith?

                             *

I've always grown
   in other people's shade.
Not for shelter
   in solidity, neither they
being spreading oak or beech nor I
   some shrinking violet

but when a face upturned
   towards frail light, a voice
that interweaves between
   dark leaves a space for
flower, path for thorn, catch something
   of light's reach and axiom

then lower on the stem
   my edges breathe, droop
through dust re-invents desire
   not for gloss but growth
from this common soil, that upward
   thrust from lateral roots

to a realm
   wholly natural, and radical.
When a face, a voice
   like new leaves on a vane
promise turn by turn
   a view, on a spiralling belt

towards that light, then
   being roused I know
while upholding the crown
   in whose shade I too
throw shadow, I draw
   a freight of light in tow.

*

. . . Human beings must be
   taught to love
silence and darkness.

But in silence comes
   the seepage of
a gas fire's breath

in darkness the pink
   of a child's
mosquito net – it seems

their very presence
   is that love
for how else can we invoke

afterworlds without
   voice, light
but through things that

breathe and move, obey
   an absence
that is deified because

absence is unbearable
   unless, in a residue
of breath and light

we bear the agony
      of presence, and do
call this bearing, loving?

                    *

Nothing can ruin the evening –
      car doors slammed, voices raised
in the last of the light, voices
      without owners. And that's
a difference between art and nature –
      art transforming – voices, traffic
tawdriness – but in a gathering-in
      an almost selfish motion; nature
extending outwards as the shore its arms
      night its stars, an open invitation.

The palace of a ship at night
      blinking stars like cursors;
those disembodied voices from
      who knows which shore, drunk –
why note them, fail them?
      Torn between life and art, why is one
without the other like a shore without its sea
      night without its stars, why am I
– still beautiful – so unable to contain
      the ugliness, my own, in either?

                    *

120

It's the eye of longing
   that I tire of
the eye of fantasy
   lost in the grey horizons.

Having neither the heart
   nor talent for
invention, why should I
   – no child of mist –

be party to this cold
   imagination, its cloak
and hood, smuggled goods
   its faery in the dingle?

Where are my sunlight's
   givens? Near the sun
and far from folk
   an albino child, skin clean

as silver, hair white as
   snow, under the Simorgh's
eye as she flies
   over the Alborz Mountains

years later will hear her cry:
   . . . behold my might,
For I have cherished thee beneath my plumes
And brought thee up among my little ones

before she ferries him home
   gives him a feather to light
as a signal
   in times of trouble.

But this is my borrowed plumage
   language, more strange to me
than this foster-tongue, this English
   fairy godmother.

*

To be so dependent on sunlight
   – small desires on the lookout
like feathers snagged on slates –
   is to be, in a climate
doomed to cloud, its changing mind
   a paler version of the story:
he whose glory flew away from him
   three times in the shape of a bird
whose wingspan was so great that rain
   could never fall but when faith
at last deserted him and falsehood
   took its place, fall it did to prove
that glory goes back to God, resides
   with God by any other name.

                            *

What is he looking for
   the great white sun
throwing the force of his search
   like torchlight onto the sea?
What he looks for
   will be present
only as long as his looking;
   what he fails to find
absent
   to the precise extent
of his brightness
   blinding himself by reflection
while the passerby takes in
   a high sun, a broken

and a peninsula of violet
   the translation between.
It's darkness
   the white sun looks for
the one thing
   by the light of his eyes
he'll never see; one thing
   the brighter, further
he throws his rays
   the more recedes: it's
his shadow that he looks for
   and will never know
if it is God or self, friend or foe
   if it follows or precedes.

*

It is said
   God created a peacock of light
and placed him
   in front of a mirror.
In the presence
   of God, being so ashamed at his own
beauty, his own
   unutterable perfection, the peacock

broke out in a sweat.
   From the sweat of his nose, God created
the Angels.
   From the sweat of his face, the Throne, Footstool
Tablet of Forms, the Pen
   the heavens and what is in them.
From breast and back
   the Visited House, prophets, holy sites, etc.

From the sweat of his two feet
    God created, from east to west, the earth.
The sea is
    glistening peacock sweat.
Tarmac too.
    From sweat of the peacock's feet of pearl
comes my window view.
    Perhaps I am formed from a trembling

drop on his ankle.
    Cypress, sunflower, bicycle wheels
grass dried in heat
    to the colour of wheat, all, all are
peacock water, peacock dew
    shame and beauty, salt and light
God's peacock
    in his consciousness, walks over.

                    *

Too much light is tiresome.
    Knowing this, today's
keeps its counsel. Tight-lipped
    the sky has closed its door
against the sea which
    like an aimless child
spreadeagles on its bed. The day
    is set aside for function.

Every shrub, roof, windowsill
    broods on its own
injunctions. Even birds on errands
    forget to play on thermals
winging it straight across the sky
    as though time and light
were the same thing, same task
    and every bird and bush accountable.

                    *

Light's sharpening
    knives of water.
I long for the coolness
    of a room downstairs.
White grapes. A morning
    cigarette. To take
umbrage behind hessian
    blow on a glass
of tea, sugarlump held
    between my teeth, taste
how bitterness
    too quickly sweetens.

Light's packed its water
    of knives in drawer
upon drawer of
    darkness. Where sea's
banded in shadow. Laid
    smaller silvers
out in the calm: glimmer
    of tines, crests
salvers and scoops, flatware
    embossed on handles.
And that downstairs room
    never to have, never to hold

the way Proust says
    on meeting with colons
that inviolate pause
    when a gathering falls silent
before it intones
    has brought him, while
reading, the scent of a rose
    which has never evaporated
though centuries old, there it comes
    with its teas and spoons
luminous fridge, against the light
    bowed silhouettes of people.

*

I've stored all the light
    I need. Stored it
in the dark jars of my body.
    Light's in its phase
of falling. Souring, sweetening.
    Boring us with its constancy

polishing, straightening. Light's
    like a grandmother tiring
pushing a strand of hair behind
    her ear, knees aching, sighing.
No one looks up, the sky's too bright.
    Four boys on seaweed ledges.

We look at the sea instead or
    inward to reservoirs
four-handled jars, fats and oils
    seven-herb pickle, smoked fish, spice
down to the cold slabs of our stores
    under bone and cartilage.

                    *

I loved you so much
    I couldn't bear the thought
of cold water on you
    dripping from your chin, hands

running down your elbow
    as you lifted your face to the sound
of footsteps. Smiled at me
    through water. Even

when the season turned
    and no one walked out of shade
to burn in sun
    you'd run the cold –

how cold your hands were.
    Nowhere, as the season turns
and I walk from shade
    or the smell of shade on a sunless

street, in and out of the shade
    of trees to find
no difference, will someone again
    bowing a silvery

head to a tap, move me
    to the kind of love that registers
on skin's temperature
    every shade of difference.

                    *

Air's utterly soft, back to its habitual
    cardigans and greys. Relief or regret?
I think of Jane, how she must have felt
    once her house was stripped of visitors.
Of myself. In days when they came en route
    to the States, Iran, bringing
their lifestyles with them. How they left.
    Leaving the house like a house

shorn of heatwave. Where a suitcase
    had been, how amplified the space.
Turmeric stains, a pot misplaced
    how aftershave can linger. And voices
of our own lives, resentful, neglected
    beginning to call from far away.
Or in another language – theirs. Crossing
    each other's waves upstairs, downstairs

making the town seem bigger, smaller
    its centre somewhere to go to
every day. Jane and all the immigrants
    whose families come to visit, overstay
their welcome, leave us holding our life
  in two cupped hands, bewildered at
its lightness, like a fledgeling's, wondering
    why it is they who have flown the nest.

                            *

And suppose I left behind
    a portrait inadvertently
like a showercap on a peg
    of this seaview that is hers
and insinuated between its clouds
    strange glimpses of myself
that would alter her view
    not only of me but of the sky
her mornings open out on or
    worse, something of herself

either way some hurt would unfold
    open out its own cloud, like smoke
would streak her air. Her air of . . .
    Seeing ourselves beautiful
also hurts. No longer what we are
    what we were we love but cannot claim.
Looking up, each time we do
    is a silver seachange pencilling
light, shading, erasing
    each time, each time a change.

And where is the singular moment
    unwritten, that's free of pain?
As if by magic, silver lines
    of the horizon have disappeared.
A black ship rides on grey.
    Between everything is a distance
by which we know ourselves, ever
    smarting in the gaps, between
clouds, ships, a child and his unseen
    parents walking on ahead.

*

'Going away'
    is not so much
a going away as a
    coming towards that

part of ourselves which
    in our daily lives
seems so curiously
    absent, distant, then here

away from home, in a snatch
    of song from a beach
at dusk, so endearingly, so
    agonizingly close.

*

Finally, in a cove
   that cups thin fog
like a hand its thirst
   this indivisibility of
sea and sky like a grey
   pearl between two claws

makes sense: as if a bay
   waisting a horizon, woman
legs twined around a man
   were what were needed
to make the horizontal
   more beautiful, more felt;

to interpose
   between the eye and sense
a possibility in containment
   of the infinite becoming part
of what the eye can never see
   but the sense can comprehend.

*

It can come from the simplest
   of things: a room
tidied, new folders slipped
   from cellophane;
how a ballpoint runs
   without smudging or
looking up through smoke
   blue spiral veils
how your eyelashes
   become nets for light
so wherever you look
   light can't escape.

What makes it shimmer?
  The irrational and static
glow that invades and
  expands a space till
like a bubble full to bursting
  poised, infrangible
skin meets the outmost
  reaches of its waves.
And the shimmering starts.
  Thickens. Radiance
solidifies to a volume
  you can walk in, wear.

Dangerous, being so sheer
  it's also safe.
You wear it like a mantle, aura
  a superstition
you must not name.
  You call it *the shining*
secretly to yourself.
  Follow it down the street
carry upstairs to unwrap
  so its perfume fills the room
like flowers waiting for water . . .
  Make it wait.

Inside its capsule, time's
  both a sentence you
must run with, grappling
  blind corners, pursuing
a flare, and a silence
  coiled, sprung to mime
every flicker and feint
  in an eye, an ear . . .
don't lag behind, don't rush it.
  All you have to go on
is how footfalls sound, shining
  dims, trust and prayer.

Who put it there? You did.
　Who can again at will?
You can. What are its talismans?
　Desire, despair. See
how it came this morning
　from loneliness, boredom
a hint of rain; a move to
　call it in as you might a boat
rise to it as if to dawn
　tell someone else what you
call it. Dare it to live up to
　rise above, such names.

What is the light we walk into
　bathe in, wake to?
Of the two lights that it is –
　one sky's, the hour's
orientation of a room
　riveting in slants, slow
pirouettes, the other –
　what is that though?
that comes to meet the first.
　As if our daily darknesses
half-felt had, sooner or later
　to see the light of day.

Our own light I mean.
　Some sleeping thing
that rises, like a fawn
　from bracken, half-dazed
at its own liquidity . . .
　what fusion is it made for?
Flesh with its source of being
　silhouette and sun
in the open hand of a clearing
　or occluded green
the heart's dissolve, to die in
　be stripped of flame?

What deaths of ego, cynicism
    cowardice must we undergo
clinging to those darknesses
    we feed like ravenous mouths
forego, to unveil the simple
    moment, that open hand
on ours, both fingering back
    the curtain to reveal
a single ray? Of truth maybe
    aligning its core between
two lights, their shining eclipsed
    as its own is newly named.

Notes and Dedications for Entries on Light